Elliott Wave Trading Mastery

Using Elliott Wave Theory with Market Trends and Indicators (MACD, RSI)

by

Nathaniel J. Brooks

DISCLAIMER

This book is only designed for educational and informational purposes. It is intended to illustrate trading ideas, systems, and market insights gained through study and practice. It is not designed to provide personalised financial guidance or suggestions.

This book does not provide any financial, investing, legal, or trading advice. All techniques, charts, examples, and scenarios are offered solely for educational illustration and should not be regarded as recommendations to buy, sell, or hold any financial asset.

Trading in the foreign exchange market and other financial instruments entails risk, including the loss of funds. No method, strategy, or example presented in this book can guarantee success. Market conditions vary, and previous performance is no guarantee of future results or illustrations.

Readers are solely responsible for their trading decisions, risk management, and outcomes. Trading should only be done with funds that you can afford to lose. Readers are encouraged to seek financial expert guidance as needed.

All chart drawings in this book are based on publicly available market price data and are intended solely as analytical examples for educational purposes. Charts, tools, platforms, brokers, and software are only mentioned for instructional purposes. The author is not

Table of Contents

INTRODUCTION

Looking at my trading screen one cold Tuesday morning in 2019, I watched the EUR/USD pair dance in what seemed like complete chaos. Price was jumping up and down, my indicators were giving mixed signals, and frankly, I was losing money faster than I cared to admit. That's when everything changed. I noticed something remarkable hiding in all that market noise - a clear, predictable pattern that would transform how I approached forex trading forever.

You've probably been there too. Staring at your charts, feeling overwhelmed by the countless indicators, conflicting signals, and the constant question: "When do I actually enter this trade?" The forex market can feel like an impossible puzzle, especially when you're trying to time your entries and exits with precision. Most traders jump from strategy to strategy, hoping the next indicator will be their holy grail. I spent three years doing exactly that until I discovered the power of Elliott Wave theory combined with two simple yet powerful indicators.

Here's what I learned during my seven years of trading forex professionally: markets don't move randomly. They follow patterns that you can learn to read like a well-written book. Elliott Wave theory reveals the natural rhythm of market psychology, while MACD and RSI act as your confirmation tools. When you combine these three elements, something magical happens - you start seeing the market's next move before it happens.

This comprehensive guide contains three interconnected books because mastering Elliott Wave trading requires a structured approach. You can't jump straight into advanced concepts without understanding the foundations, just like you wouldn't attempt to run a marathon without first learning to walk. Book One builds your Elliott Wave foundation with real examples from my trading journal. Book Two shows you exactly how to integrate MACD and RSI with your wave analysis - this is where most traders see their breakthrough moment. Book Three takes you to professional-level application, including the risk management principles that have kept me profitable through market crashes and boom periods alike.

I remember my first successful Elliott Wave trade on GBP/JPY. After months of studying wave patterns, I spotted a textbook wave 3 formation. MACD confirmed the momentum, RSI showed we weren't overbought yet, and I entered the trade with complete confidence. That single trade netted me more profit than my previous month of random indicator chasing. More importantly, it proved that systematic analysis beats gut feelings every time.

By the time you finish these three books, you'll possess a complete trading system that works in trending markets, ranging markets, and everything in between. You'll know exactly when to enter trades, where to place your stops, and how to maximize your profits using wave targets. Most importantly, you'll trade with the confidence that comes from understanding why the market moves the way it does.

BOOK 1
Elliott Wave Foundations in Forex

Understanding the Core Principles and Basic Wave Patterns

CHAPTER 1

The DNA of Market Movement - Understanding Elliott Wave Theory

The currency markets have been my teacher for over eight years now, and through countless hours of chart analysis, I've learned that price movements aren't random chaos. They follow predictable patterns rooted in human psychology. When you understand these patterns, trading transforms from gambling to systematic analysis.

What Elliott Wave Theory Reveals About Market Psychology

Ralph Nelson Elliott discovered something profound in the 1930s that still drives forex markets today. Every time traders become optimistic about a currency pair, they create buying pressure. When fear takes over, selling dominates. This emotional cycle repeats endlessly, creating wave-like patterns that you can learn to identify and trade profitably.

The beauty of Elliott Wave theory lies in its simplicity. Human emotions swing between two extremes: greed and fear. These emotions don't change randomly - they follow predictable sequences. When EUR/USD starts trending upward, initial buyers create the first wave. Profit-taking causes a pullback. Then more buyers jump in, creating an even stronger wave. This psychological dance continues in measurable patterns.

Chart 1: EUR/USD daily chart showing a complete 8-wave Elliott Wave cycle

You'll notice that waves aren't all the same size or duration. That's because market participants react differently at various stages of a trend. Early adopters move first, creating smaller waves. When the mainstream catches on, the waves become more powerful. Finally, when everyone's already bought in, the trend exhausts itself.

The 8-Wave Cycle: How Markets Breathe and Move

Every complete Elliott Wave sequence contains eight waves that tell a story. The first five waves move in the direction of the main trend - we call this the impulse phase. Waves 1, 3, and 5 push prices forward, while waves 2 and 4 provide necessary corrections. Then comes a three-wave corrective phase labeled A, B, and C that moves against the main trend.

This isn't just theory - it's how markets actually function. During my trading career, I've watched this pattern play out hundreds of times across major currency pairs. The most reliable profits come from identifying where you are in this 8-wave sequence and positioning accordingly.

Wave 1 typically starts quietly. Most traders miss it because it looks like just another small move. Wave 2 can retrace deeply, often wiping out newcomers who jumped in late. Wave 3 is where the magic happens - it's usually the longest and strongest wave, where serious money gets made. Wave 4 provides another correction, but it rarely goes as deep as wave 2. Wave 5 completes the impulse, though it sometimes shows signs of weakness.

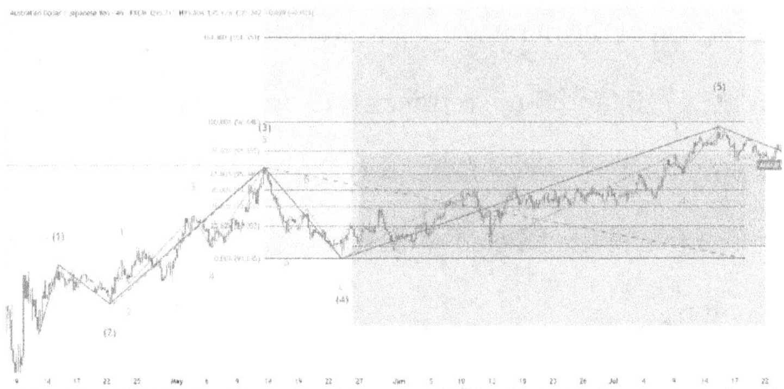

Chart 2: 4-hour chart displaying a textbook 5-wave impulse sequence with Fibonacci retracement levels showing typical wave 2 and wave 4 correction depths

The corrective phase tells its own story. Wave A often catches traders off guard because they expect the trend to continue. Wave B can be tricky - it sometimes retraces significantly, making traders think the trend is resuming. Wave C usually provides the final washout before a new impulse sequence begins.

Why Forex Markets Are Perfect for Elliott Wave Analysis

Currency markets possess unique characteristics that make Elliott Wave analysis exceptionally effective. Unlike stocks, which can be influenced by company-specific news, forex pairs reflect the economic relationship between two entire countries. This creates cleaner, more predictable wave patterns.

The 24-hour nature of forex markets also helps. There's no overnight gap risk that can disrupt wave counts. Trends develop smoothly, and corrections unfold logically. Additionally, the massive liquidity in major pairs like EUR/USD, GBP/USD, and USD/JPY prevents artificial price manipulations that might distort wave structures.

I've found that weekly and daily timeframes work exceptionally well for Elliott Wave analysis in forex. Monthly charts reveal the major wave cycles that can last for years, while hourly charts help with precise entry and exit timing.

Chart 3: USD/CHF weekly chart showing a multi-year Elliott Wave cycle with each major wave clearly labeled and trend lines connecting significant pivot points

Central bank interventions and economic announcements do impact wave structures, but they rarely invalidate the overall pattern. Instead, they often accelerate wave development or create the catalyst for wave completions.

Building Your Elliott Wave Foundation

Learning to identify Elliott Waves requires patience and practice. Start by studying completed wave sequences on historical charts. This trains your eye to recognize the natural flow of market psychology. Once you can spot finished patterns consistently, you'll develop the confidence to analyze developing waves in real-time.

The key is understanding that Elliott Wave analysis is both an art and a science. The rules provide structure, but successful application requires developing an intuitive feel for market rhythm. This comes only through experience and careful observation of how waves actually unfold in live trading conditions.

Your journey into Elliott Wave mastery begins with accepting that markets have memory and patterns. Price doesn't move randomly - it moves in response to collective human psychology, and those psychological responses follow predictable sequences that you can learn to read and trade profitably.

CHAPTER 2

Decoding the 5-Wave Impulse Pattern

The 5-wave impulse pattern forms the backbone of every major forex trend. When you master this pattern, you'll recognize the most profitable trading opportunities in the currency markets. These five waves represent the natural progression of human psychology during trending periods, and understanding each wave's characteristics will transform how you approach trade entries and exits.

The Anatomy of Trending Moves in Currency Pairs

Every significant trend in forex begins with a 5-wave impulse sequence. This isn't just a theoretical concept - it's the actual structure that price follows when markets move decisively in one direction. The pattern consists of three advancing waves separated by two corrective waves, creating a rhythm that reflects how traders psychologically process trending markets.

Wave structures in forex pairs like EUR/USD or GBP/JPY develop differently than in other markets because currencies represent economic relationships between countries. When economic fundamentals favor one currency over another, the resulting trends often produce textbook 5-wave patterns that can last for weeks or months.

During my years analyzing forex charts, I've noticed that major currency pairs tend to produce cleaner wave patterns than exotic pairs. This happens because major pairs have higher liquidity and more efficient price discovery, which allows natural wave structures to develop without interference from irregular trading volumes.

Chart 4: EUR/USD daily chart showing a complete 5-wave upward impulse with each wave clearly labeled and trend channel lines connecting the wave highs and lows

The beauty of the 5-wave pattern lies in its predictability once you understand the psychological drivers. Each wave serves a specific purpose in the overall trend development, and recognizing these purposes helps you determine where price is likely to head next.

Identifying Waves 1, 3, and 5: The Power Waves

Waves 1, 3, and 5 are the driving forces of any impulse pattern. These waves move in the direction of the main trend and represent periods when bulls or bears are in complete control. Each power wave has distinct characteristics that help you identify them on your charts.

Wave 1 often begins quietly and can be difficult to distinguish from random price movement. Many traders miss wave 1 entirely because it doesn't stand out until the pattern completes. However, wave 1 sets the foundation for everything that follows. It represents the first group of traders recognizing a new trend opportunity.

Wave 3 typically becomes the most powerful and extended wave in the entire sequence. This wave develops when the broader trading community recognizes the trend and jumps on board. The psychological momentum during wave 3 creates strong, sustained price movement that often exceeds trader expectations. In forex markets, wave

3 frequently produces the clearest and most profitable trading signals.

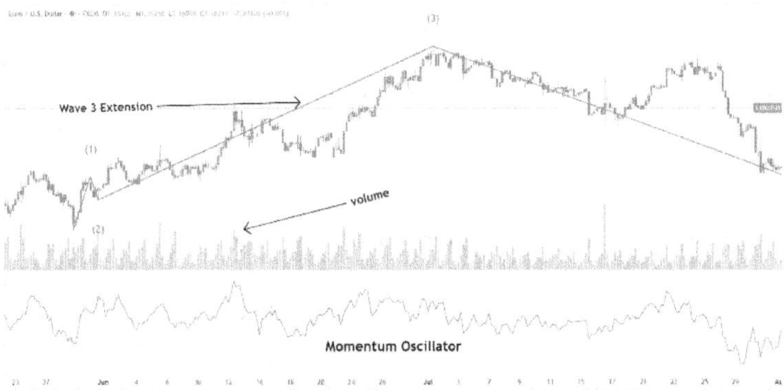

Chart 5: 4-hour chart displaying wave 3 extension with volume indicators showing increased trading activity and momentum oscillators confirming strong directional bias

Wave 5 completes the impulse pattern but often shows signs of exhaustion. By the time wave 5 develops, most traders have already positioned themselves in the trend direction. This wave sometimes fails to exceed the wave 3 high, creating what we call a truncated fifth wave. Smart traders watch for divergence signals during wave 5 development.

You'll find that power waves in forex pairs respond well to Fibonacci projections. Wave 3 often extends 1.618 times the length of wave 1, while wave 5 frequently equals wave 1 in length or extends to 0.618 times the combined length of waves 1 through 3.

Recognizing Waves 2 and 4: The Correction Phases

Corrective waves 2 and 4 serve essential functions in the impulse pattern by allowing the market to digest gains and prepare for the next advance. These waves represent profit-taking periods and temporary shifts in sentiment that actually strengthen the overall trend.

Wave 2 corrections can be particularly deep, sometimes retracing up to 78.6% of wave 1's advance. This deep retracement often shakes out weak-handed traders and creates the foundation for a powerful wave 3. When I first started trading Elliott Waves, I made the mistake of assuming wave 2 corrections meant the trend was over. Experience taught me that deep wave 2 retracements often precede the strongest wave 3 movements.

Wave 4 corrections typically remain more shallow than wave 2, usually retracing between 23.6% and 38.2% of wave 3's movement. This alternation between deep and shallow corrections helps maintain the overall trend momentum while providing natural entry points for traders who missed earlier opportunities.

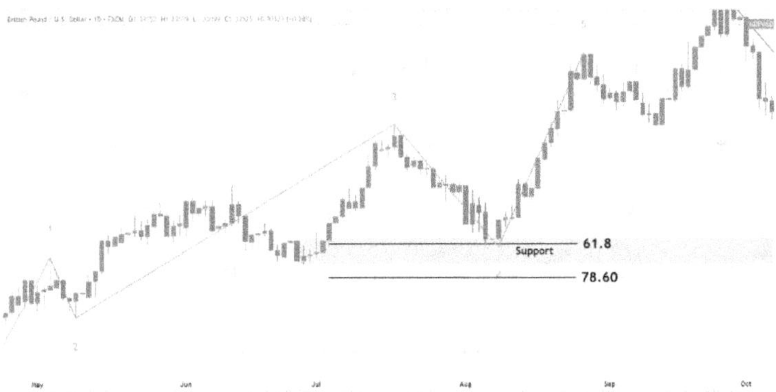

Chart 6: chart showing alternating wave 2 and wave 4 corrections with Fibonacci retracement levels marking typical correction zones and support/resistance areas

The corrective waves also follow specific rules that help validate your wave count. Wave 2 cannot retrace below the starting point of wave 1, and wave 4 cannot overlap with wave 1's price territory except in rare diagonal patterns.

Real Trading Story: Catching a Perfect 5-Wave Move on EUR/USD

Last autumn, I was monitoring EUR/USD when it started showing signs of a completed corrective phase. The pair had been declining for several weeks, but the selling pressure was beginning to fade. I noticed what appeared to be the beginning of wave 1 in a new upward impulse.

The initial move was modest - only about 50 pips - but it had the characteristics of a genuine wave 1. After a textbook wave 2 correction that retraced 61.8% of the initial advance, I prepared for what could be a powerful wave 3. The correction found support exactly where Elliott Wave theory suggested it should.

When wave 3 began developing, the momentum was unmistakable. Price moved steadily higher over several days, eventually extending to 1.618 times the length of wave 1. The wave 4 correction was shallow, retracing only 23.6% of wave 3, which maintained the bullish momentum perfectly.

Wave 5 completed the pattern by reaching the projected target area, giving me a complete 5-wave sequence that provided multiple trading opportunities. This experience reinforced how powerful Elliott Wave analysis can be when you understand each wave's psychological foundation and respect the pattern's natural development.

Understanding 5-wave impulse patterns gives you a roadmap for trending markets. When you can identify which wave is developing, you gain tremendous insight into where price is likely to move next and how strong that movement might be.

CHAPTER 3
Mastering Corrective Wave Patterns

Corrective waves are where most traders lose money, yet they offer some of the best trading opportunities once you understand their structure. While impulse waves capture the headlines with their dramatic price movements, corrective patterns provide the foundation for future trends and create ideal entry points for patient traders.

The ABC Correction: Market's Way of Taking a Breather

The most fundamental corrective pattern consists of three waves labeled A, B, and C. This structure appears repeatedly across all timeframes in forex trading and represents the market's natural way of digesting previous gains or losses before resuming the main trend.

Wave A typically catches traders off guard because it moves against the prevailing trend when most participants expect continuation. During my early trading years, I often mistook the start of wave A for just a minor pullback, only to watch it develop into a significant correction. This wave usually unfolds in five smaller sub-waves, indicating genuine selling pressure rather than mere profit-taking.

Wave B creates the most confusion among traders because it moves back in the direction of the original trend. Many inexperienced traders see wave B as confirmation that the trend is resuming, leading them to enter positions just before wave C devastates their accounts. Wave B typically retraces between 38.2% and 78.6% of wave A's movement, though it can occasionally exceed wave A's starting point in complex corrections.

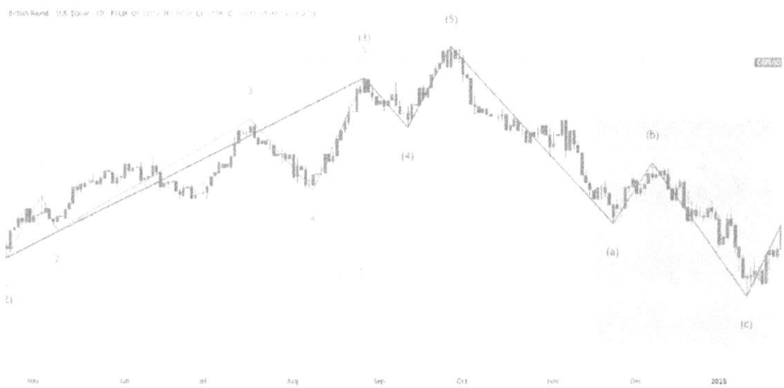

Chart 7: GBP/USD daily chart showing a complete ABC correction

Wave C usually provides the most decisive movement within the corrective sequence. This wave often equals wave A in length or extends to 1.618 times wave A's distance. The completion of wave C signals the end of the corrective phase and often sets up excellent trading opportunities in the direction of the larger trend.

Understanding ABC corrections helps you avoid the psychological trap of fighting the market during consolidation periods. Instead of viewing corrections as obstacles, you can use them as opportunities to position yourself advantageously for the next impulse wave.

Complex Corrections: When Markets Get Tricky

Not all corrections follow the simple ABC pattern. Markets sometimes develop complex corrective structures that combine multiple ABC sequences or create unique patterns that test your analytical skills. These complex corrections often occur when market sentiment remains unclear or when fundamental factors create conflicting pressures.

Double corrections consist of two ABC patterns connected by an intervening wave labeled X. The notation becomes WXY, where W and Y represent ABC corrections and X serves as a connecting wave. These patterns frequently develop in forex markets when economic data creates mixed signals about a currency's prospects.

Triple corrections add another layer of complexity with a WXYXZ structure. While less common than double corrections, they do occur in major currency pairs during periods of economic uncertainty. The EUR/USD pair demonstrated a textbook triple correction during the European debt crisis, creating extended sideways movement that frustrated trend-following traders.

Complex corrections require patience and careful analysis. The key is recognizing that these patterns will eventually resolve, typically leading to strong impulse moves once the market clarifies its direction. During complex corrections, I focus on identifying the overall correction boundaries rather than trying to trade every sub-wave movement.

Flat, Zigzag, and Triangle Patterns in Forex

Corrective patterns come in three main varieties, each with distinct characteristics that influence how they develop and resolve. Recognizing these patterns helps you anticipate both the duration and the likely conclusion of corrective phases.

Zigzag corrections create sharp, decisive moves that quickly retrace significant portions of the previous impulse wave. In a zigzag, wave A and wave C are both five-wave structures, while wave B forms a three-wave pattern. These corrections typically retrace 50% to 78.6% of the preceding impulse and resolve relatively quickly.

Flat corrections develop more gradually and usually indicate underlying strength in the main trend direction. Wave A forms a three-wave structure, wave B retraces most or all of wave A, and wave C typically equals wave A in length. Flats often occur as wave 4 corrections in strong trends, suggesting the trend will resume with minimal retracement.

Chart 8: chart showing a contracting triangle correction with converging trend lines and decreasing wave amplitude leading to a breakout continuation

Triangle corrections appear as sideways consolidation patterns with converging price action. These patterns consist of five waves labeled ABCDE, with each wave typically forming a three-wave sub-structure. Triangles usually occur in wave 4 positions or as wave B within larger corrections. When triangles complete, they often lead to sharp breakout moves that equal the triangle's widest point.

The key to trading corrective patterns successfully is recognizing that they serve a purpose in the larger wave structure. Rather than fighting these patterns, you can use them to prepare for the next trending phase.

Personal Experience: How I Learned to Wait for Corrections

Early in my trading career, I consistently lost money trying to pick tops and bottoms during corrective phases. I would see what looked like wave A completing and immediately assume the correction was over, only to get caught in wave C's final decline.

The breakthrough came when I started treating corrections as complete patterns rather than individual waves. Instead of trying to catch every bounce, I learned to wait for clear evidence that the entire corrective sequence had finished. This meant missing some early entries but avoiding the significant losses that come from mistiming corrective waves.

I developed a systematic approach to correction analysis that focuses on three key factors: the correction's relationship to the preceding impulse, the internal structure of each corrective wave, and the overall time proportion compared to the trending phases. This approach transformed corrections from trading obstacles into opportunities.

The most profitable trades often develop immediately after complex corrections complete. The market tends to move decisively once the corrective uncertainty resolves, creating powerful trending moves that reward patient traders who waited for clear signals rather than gambling on correction timing.

CONCLUSION

Your Foundation is Set - Moving Forward with Confidence

You now possess the fundamental knowledge that separates successful Elliott Wave traders from those who struggle with market timing. The concepts we've covered in this first book form the bedrock of everything you'll learn moving forward. Understanding wave psychology, recognizing impulse patterns, and identifying corrective structures gives you a significant advantage over traders who rely solely on lagging indicators.

The Power of Pattern Recognition

Elliott Wave theory works in forex markets because it reflects the unchanging nature of human psychology. Fear and greed drive market participants today just as they did decades ago when Ralph Elliott first documented these patterns. When you see a five-wave impulse developing on EUR/USD, you're witnessing the same psychological progression that has repeated countless times throughout market history.

The patterns you've learned aren't just theoretical constructs - they're practical tools that help you anticipate market behavior. Wave 3 will almost always be the strongest wave in an impulse sequence because that's when the majority of traders recognize the trend and jump aboard. Wave 4 corrections will typically remain shallow because the underlying trend momentum remains strong. These aren't coincidences - they're predictable outcomes based on crowd psychology.

Chart 9: weekly chart showing multiple complete Elliott Wave cycles over a two-year period with each 8-wave sequence clearly labeled and trend channels marking major wave boundaries

Your ability to recognize these patterns will improve with practice and experience. Start by analyzing completed wave sequences on historical charts before attempting to identify developing patterns in real-time. This approach builds your pattern recognition skills without the pressure of live trading decisions.

Building Confidence Through Understanding

Confidence in trading comes from understanding why markets move the way they do rather than simply following mechanical rules. When you understand that corrective waves serve a purpose in preparing for the next impulse, you stop fearing pullbacks and start viewing them as opportunities. This psychological shift transforms your entire approach to market analysis.

The wave counting rules and guidelines we've discussed provide structure to your analysis, but they also require interpretation and judgment. Markets occasionally produce patterns that challenge traditional wave counts, and your success depends on maintaining flexibility while respecting the underlying principles. Experience will teach you when to stick with your original count and when to consider alternative interpretations.

During my years of trading Elliott Waves, I've learned that the most profitable trades often come from the simplest, most obvious patterns. Complex wave structures can be intellectually satisfying to analyze, but they rarely provide the clearest trading signals. Focus on developing mastery of basic patterns before attempting to decode intricate corrective sequences.

The Importance of Timeframe Analysis

Elliott Wave patterns manifest across all timeframes simultaneously, creating a hierarchical structure that provides multiple layers of analysis. A wave 3 on the daily chart might contain five complete waves when viewed on the hourly timeframe. This fractal nature of Elliott Waves gives you tremendous flexibility in timing your trades while maintaining consistency with the larger trend direction.

Learning to synchronize your analysis across different timeframes will become crucial as you advance in your Elliott Wave education. The weekly chart provides context for major wave positions, daily charts help identify intermediate-term patterns, and hourly charts assist with precise entry and exit timing.

Never lose sight of the bigger picture when analyzing shorter timeframes. A perfect five-wave pattern on the 15-minute chart means little if it's developing as a small subwave within a larger corrective sequence. Always work from longer timeframes down to shorter ones to maintain proper perspective.

Preparing for Advanced Concepts

The foundation you've built through understanding basic Elliott Wave principles prepares you for the advanced concepts we'll explore in the next two books. You'll learn to combine wave analysis with technical indicators like MACD and RSI, creating a comprehensive trading system that provides both direction and timing signals.

The integration of technical indicators with Elliott Wave analysis doesn't complicate the process - it clarifies it. MACD can confirm wave momentum while RSI helps identify wave exhaustion points. These tools work together to increase your confidence in wave counts and improve your trade timing.

Risk management becomes more precise when you understand wave structures. Elliott Wave theory provides natural stop-loss levels and profit targets based on wave relationships and Fibonacci ratios. This systematic approach to position management reduces emotional decision-making and improves overall trading results.

Your Next Steps Forward

Practice applying these concepts to current market conditions before moving to the next book. Spend time identifying wave patterns on different currency pairs and timeframes. Keep a trading journal documenting your wave counts and observations - this will accelerate your learning process significantly.

The journey to Elliott Wave mastery requires patience and persistence. Some patterns will challenge your analysis, and some wave counts will prove incorrect. This is part of the learning process that every successful Elliott Wave trader experiences. Each mistake teaches valuable lessons that improve your future analysis.

Your foundation in Elliott Wave theory is now solid enough to support the advanced techniques and integration strategies we'll explore next. You understand how markets move, why they move that way, and how to identify the patterns that repeat endlessly across all timeframes. This knowledge transforms you from a reactive trader into a proactive analyst who anticipates market behavior rather than simply responding to it.

BOOK 2

Technical Integration Mastery

Combining Elliott Waves with MACD and RSI for Powerful Signals

CHAPTER 1
MACD - Your Wave Confirmation Partner

The Moving Average Convergence Divergence indicator serves as one of the most reliable confirmation tools for Elliott Wave analysis in forex trading. When you combine MACD signals with your wave counts, you create a powerful system that increases accuracy while reducing false signals. This partnership between wave theory and momentum indicators transforms guesswork into systematic analysis.

Understanding MACD Basics in Simple Terms

MACD consists of three components that work together to reveal momentum changes in currency pairs. The MACD line represents the difference between a 12-period exponential moving average and a 26-period exponential moving average. The signal line is a 9-period exponential moving average of the MACD line itself. The histogram shows the difference between these two lines, providing the earliest indication of momentum shifts.

The indicator oscillates above and below a zero line, creating clear visual signals about trend strength and direction. When MACD trades above zero, it indicates that shorter-term momentum favors the upside. Below zero suggests downward momentum dominates. However, the most valuable signals come from the crossovers and divergences that align with Elliott Wave patterns.

MACD works exceptionally well in trending markets, which makes it perfect for confirming Elliott Wave impulse patterns. During strong trends, MACD maintains its directional bias while providing early warnings when momentum begins to fade. This characteristic helps you identify when wave sequences might be completing or when corrective phases are beginning.

Chart 10: chart showing MACD indicator below price action with MACD line, signal line, and histogram clearly labeled during a 5-wave impulse sequence

The beauty of MACD lies in its simplicity and reliability. Unlike oscillators that can remain overbought or oversold for extended periods, MACD provides clear directional signals that align naturally with Elliott Wave principles. When wave 3 develops its characteristic strength, MACD typically shows strong momentum in the trend direction.

As wave 5 completes, MACD often begins showing signs of weakening momentum.

How MACD Divergence Reveals Wave Weakness

Divergence occurs when price action and MACD momentum move in opposite directions, creating one of the most reliable warning signals in technical analysis. When combined with Elliott Wave theory, divergence patterns become even more powerful because you can anticipate where they're most likely to occur.

Bearish divergence develops when price makes higher highs while MACD forms lower highs. This pattern frequently appears as wave 5 completes in an uptrend, warning that the impulse pattern is losing momentum. The divergence doesn't predict exact timing, but it alerts you that the trend is becoming vulnerable to reversal.

Bullish divergence creates the opposite scenario, with price making lower lows while MACD forms higher lows.

This pattern often appears as corrective waves complete, particularly during the final stages of wave C in ABC corrections. The divergence suggests that selling pressure is diminishing and that a new impulse wave might be beginning.

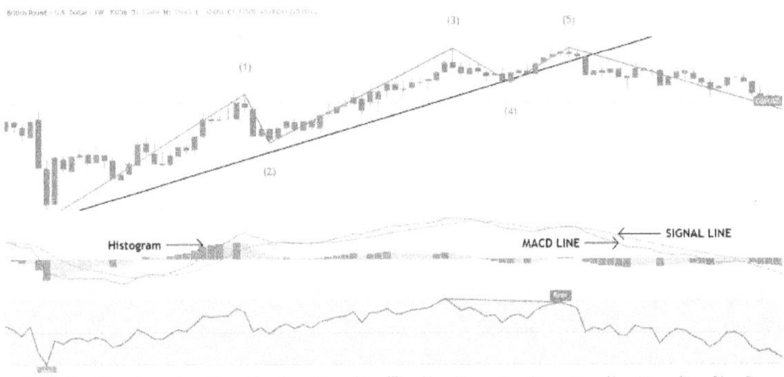

Chart 11: chart displaying bearish divergence between price highs and MACD highs during wave 5 completion with trend lines connecting the divergent peaks

The most reliable divergences occur across multiple timeframes. When both daily and 4-hour charts show divergence patterns coinciding with potential wave completions, the signal strength increases dramatically. I've found that divergence patterns appearing at natural

Elliott Wave completion points provide some of the highest probability trading setups.

Hidden divergence patterns offer additional confirmation for trend continuation. Hidden bullish divergence occurs when price makes higher lows while MACD makes lower lows, often appearing during wave 4 corrections in strong uptrends. Hidden bearish divergence shows price making lower highs while MACD makes higher highs, frequently occurring during wave 4 corrections in downtrends.

Timing Wave Entries with MACD Crossovers

MACD crossover signals provide excellent timing tools for Elliott Wave entries when used correctly. The signal line crossover occurs when the MACD line crosses above or below the 9-period signal line, indicating momentum changes that often coincide with wave developments.

Bullish crossovers work best when they occur during corrective wave completions, particularly as wave 2 or wave 4 corrections end. The crossover doesn't guarantee that the correction has finished, but it suggests that momentum is shifting back toward the trend direction. Combined with proper wave counting, these crossovers can help you enter new positions near the beginning of powerful wave 3 advances.

Zero line crossovers provide stronger signals because they indicate that momentum has shifted from negative to positive or vice versa. When MACD crosses above zero during what appears to be a wave 1 development, it confirms that new bullish momentum is building. Conversely, zero line crosses to the downside often coincide with the beginning of significant corrective phases.

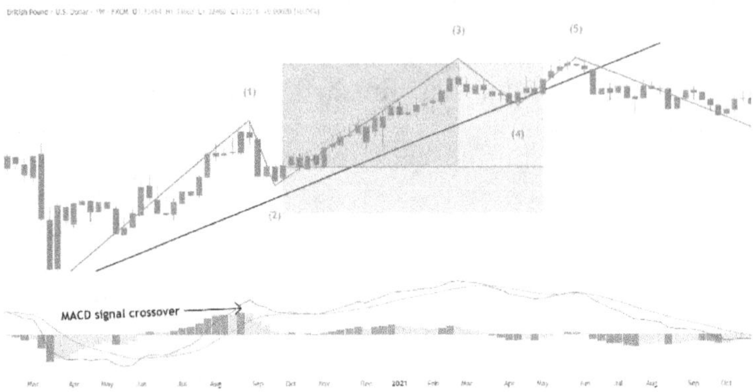

Chart 12: chart showing MACD crossover signals aligned with Elliott Wave turning points, highlighting successful entry opportunities at wave 2 and wave 4 completions

The histogram provides the earliest crossover signals because it shows the relationship between the MACD line and signal line before they actually cross. When the histogram starts moving toward zero from negative territory, it warns that a bullish crossover is approaching. This early warning system helps you prepare for potential wave completions before they become obvious to other traders.

Trading Story: When MACD Saved Me From a False Wave 5

During the spring of 2021, I was analyzing what appeared to be a developing wave 5 in USD/CAD. The pair had completed what looked like waves 1 through 4 of an impulse pattern, and price was pushing toward new highs in what should have been the final wave. My wave count suggested significant upside potential remained.

However, MACD was telling a different story. While price reached new highs, MACD failed to confirm the advance, creating clear bearish divergence. The divergence pattern was particularly pronounced on both the daily and 4-hour timeframes, which heightened my concerns about the wave count.

Instead of entering a long position based solely on the Elliott Wave pattern, I waited for additional confirmation. The MACD histogram began declining even as price continued higher, suggesting that momentum was weakening significantly. Within days, what I thought was wave 5 turned out to be a false breakout, and the pair reversed sharply into a corrective phase.

This experience reinforced the value of combining Elliott Wave analysis with momentum confirmation. MACD doesn't just confirm your wave counts - it can warn you when patterns aren't developing as expected. The indicator's ability to reveal momentum divergences often prevents costly mistakes that pure wave counting might miss.

Building MACD Into Your Wave Analysis

Integrating MACD into your Elliott Wave analysis requires understanding how momentum typically develops during different wave phases. Wave 1 often shows initial momentum building as MACD crosses above zero. Wave 3 displays the strongest MACD momentum, often with the steepest histogram readings. Wave 5 frequently shows momentum divergence, warning of impending trend completion.

Corrective waves create their own MACD patterns. Wave A corrections often push MACD below zero, while wave B bounces can create temporary bullish crossovers. Wave C completions frequently coincide with MACD reaching extreme readings before momentum begins to shift back toward the main trend direction.

The key is viewing MACD as a confirmation tool rather than a standalone trading system. Your Elliott Wave count provides the framework for understanding market structure, while MACD confirms whether momentum supports your wave interpretation. This combination creates a robust analytical approach that improves both accuracy and timing in your forex trading decisions.

CHAPTER 2

RSI - The Wave Momentum Detective

The Relative Strength Index serves as your early warning system for wave exhaustion and reversal points in forex trading. While MACD excels at confirming trend direction and momentum shifts, RSI specializes in identifying when waves are approaching completion due to overbought or oversold conditions. This makes RSI an invaluable partner for Elliott Wave analysis.

RSI Fundamentals Every Wave Trader Needs to Know

RSI measures the speed and magnitude of price changes over a specific period, typically 14 periods. The indicator oscillates between 0 and 100, with readings above 70 traditionally considered overbought and readings below 30 deemed oversold. However, these traditional levels require adjustment when analyzing Elliott Wave patterns in trending forex markets.

The calculation compares average gains to average losses over the chosen period, creating a momentum oscillator that reveals the internal strength or weakness of price movements. When RSI climbs toward extreme levels, it suggests that the current price movement is becoming unsustainable. Conversely, RSI readings near extreme lows indicate that selling pressure may be exhausting itself.

In strongly trending markets, RSI can remain in overbought or oversold territory for extended periods. This characteristic initially frustrated me until I learned to adjust my interpretation based on the Elliott Wave context. During wave 3 developments, RSI often stays overbought for weeks while the trend maintains its strength. The key is understanding when these extreme readings signal wave completion versus trend continuation.

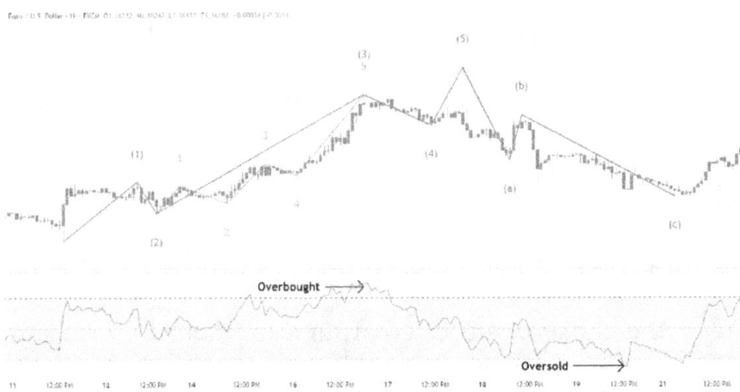

Chart 13: chart showing RSI indicator with overbought and oversold zones marked, displaying how RSI behavior differs during various Elliott Wave phases

RSI works particularly well on shorter timeframes for precise entry timing while longer timeframes provide context about major wave developments. The 4-hour RSI helps identify intraday wave completions, while daily RSI reveals intermediate-term exhaustion points that often coincide with significant wave turning points.

Identifying Wave Exhaustion with RSI Extremes

Extreme RSI readings become most significant when they occur at logical Elliott Wave completion points. Wave 5 endings frequently coincide with RSI reaching overbought extremes above 80, particularly when combined with negative divergence patterns. These extreme readings suggest that buying enthusiasm has reached unsustainable levels.

During corrective phases, RSI extremes help identify potential wave C completion points. When RSI drops below 20 during what appears to be a final corrective wave, it often signals that selling pressure is becoming exhausted. This information proves invaluable for timing entries at the beginning of new impulse sequences.

The duration RSI spends in extreme territory also provides clues about wave development. Brief spikes above 80 or below 20 often indicate temporary exhaustion that leads to minor corrections. Extended periods in extreme territory typically suggest more significant wave completions that lead to substantial reversals or corrective phases.

Context becomes crucial when interpreting RSI extremes. An RSI reading of 75 might signal exhaustion during a wave 1 development but could indicate normal strength during a powerful wave 3 advance. Understanding where you are in the Elliott Wave sequence helps you interpret RSI readings more accurately and avoid premature exit signals.

RSI Divergence: The Early Warning System

RSI divergence patterns provide some of the most reliable signals for anticipating Elliott Wave completions. Bearish divergence occurs when price makes higher highs while RSI forms lower highs, creating a warning that momentum is failing to support continued price advance. This pattern frequently appears as wave 5 develops in impulse sequences.

The most significant bearish divergences develop across multiple swing highs rather than just two points. When RSI consistently fails to confirm new price highs over several weeks or months, it creates a powerful warning that a major wave sequence is approaching completion. I've found that these extended divergence patterns often precede the most significant trend reversals.

Bullish divergence creates the opposite pattern, with price making lower lows while RSI forms higher lows. This divergence often appears during the final stages of corrective waves, particularly as wave C approaches completion in ABC corrections. The pattern suggests that selling pressure is diminishing even though price continues declining.

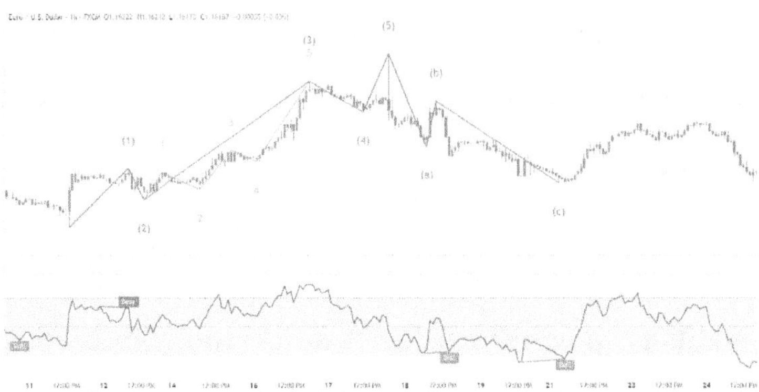

Chart 14: chart showing multiple bearish divergence signals between price peaks and RSI peaks during an extended wave 5 development with trend lines connecting the divergent points

Hidden divergence patterns provide additional confirmation for trend continuation within Elliott Wave contexts. Hidden bullish divergence occurs when price makes higher lows while RSI makes lower lows, often appearing during wave 4 corrections in strong uptrends. This pattern suggests that the underlying trend remains strong despite temporary weakness.

Class A divergences occur when RSI reaches extreme levels while creating the divergence pattern. These provide the strongest signals because they combine momentum exhaustion with divergence warnings. Class B divergences develop without extreme RSI readings, making them less reliable but still valuable for confirming wave analysis.

Personal Account: How RSI Helped Me Spot a Major Wave 3

In the autumn of 2020, I was monitoring EUR/JPY after identifying what appeared to be a completed ABC correction. The pair had declined significantly over several months, but the selling momentum was beginning to fade. RSI had reached oversold levels below 25 and was starting to form higher lows while price continued making lower lows.

This bullish divergence pattern caught my attention because it was developing at what I believed was the end of a corrective wave C. The Elliott Wave count suggested that a new impulse sequence should begin soon, and RSI was confirming that selling pressure was exhausting itself. When RSI finally crossed back above 30, it provided confirmation that momentum was shifting.

The subsequent wave 3 development exceeded my expectations, with EUR/JPY advancing over 800 pips during the following six weeks. RSI remained in overbought territory for most of this advance, which initially concerned me until I realized this was normal behavior during powerful wave 3 movements. The indicator stayed above 60 throughout the advance, confirming the strength of the trending momentum.

What made this trade particularly successful was recognizing that RSI extremes have different meanings depending on the Elliott Wave context. The initial oversold reading signaled exhaustion of the corrective phase, while the subsequent overbought readings confirmed the power of the new impulse wave.

Combining RSI with Wave Structure Analysis

RSI becomes most powerful when integrated with proper Elliott Wave structure analysis rather than used as a standalone indicator. The oscillator helps confirm what your wave count already suggests while providing additional timing precision for entries and exits.

During impulse wave development, RSI typically shows distinct patterns for each wave. Wave 1 often pushes RSI from neutral territory toward the first extreme reading. Wave 2 corrections usually bring RSI back toward the opposite extreme. Wave 3 frequently maintains RSI in trending territory for extended periods. Wave 4 corrections typically create more moderate RSI retracements than wave 2. Wave 5 often shows RSI divergence as momentum begins to fade.

Corrective waves create their own RSI signatures. Simple ABC corrections often show RSI reaching one extreme during wave A, recovering during wave B, and reaching a more significant extreme during wave C. Complex corrections can create multiple RSI swings that help identify the various sub-components of the corrective sequence.

The key to successful RSI integration is maintaining proper perspective about timeframes and wave degrees. A 15-minute RSI extreme means little if it occurs within a minor subwave of a larger pattern. Focus on RSI signals that align with significant wave turning points on appropriate timeframes for your trading style.

Understanding RSI behavior during different Elliott Wave phases transforms this simple oscillator into a sophisticated timing tool. When RSI confirms your wave analysis, it increases confidence in your trading decisions. When RSI contradicts your wave count, it warns you to reconsider your interpretation before committing capital to questionable patterns.

CHAPTER 3

The Triple Confirmation Strategy

Combining Elliott Wave analysis with MACD and RSI creates a comprehensive trading system that significantly improves your success rate in forex markets. This triple confirmation approach eliminates many false signals while providing clear entry and exit criteria based on multiple forms of market analysis working in harmony.

Elliott Wave + MACD + RSI = Trading Edge

The power of this combination lies in how each component addresses different aspects of market analysis. Elliott Wave theory provides the structural framework by identifying where price is likely headed based on pattern completion. MACD confirms momentum and trend direction while revealing divergence patterns that warn of potential reversals. RSI adds precise timing by identifying overbought and oversold conditions that often coincide with wave completions.

When all three elements align, they create high-probability trading opportunities that offer excellent risk-reward ratios. Elliott Wave analysis tells you what should happen next, MACD confirms that momentum supports your expectation, and RSI helps you time your entry when market conditions are optimal.

The beauty of this system becomes apparent during wave 3 developments. Your Elliott Wave count identifies the potential for a strong trending move, MACD shows building momentum with bullish crossovers, and RSI confirms that market conditions haven't reached exhaustion levels yet. This convergence of signals provides confidence to enter trades with larger position sizes and hold them longer for maximum profit potential.

During corrective phases, the triple confirmation system helps you avoid premature entries while identifying optimal positioning for the next trending phase. Wave analysis helps you understand the correction's likely duration and depth, MACD reveals when momentum begins shifting back toward the main trend, and RSI shows when selling or buying pressure reaches exhaustion levels.

Setting Up Your Charts for Maximum Clarity

Proper chart setup becomes crucial when managing multiple forms of analysis simultaneously. I recommend using a three-panel layout with price action and Elliott Wave annotations on the main chart, MACD in the middle panel, and RSI in the bottom panel. This arrangement allows you to quickly assess all three components without switching between different chart views.

Color coding enhances visual analysis significantly. Use consistent colors for bullish and bearish signals across all indicators. When MACD shows bullish momentum, RSI indicates favorable conditions, and your Elliott Wave count suggests upward movement, the visual harmony reinforces the signal strength and builds trading confidence.

Timeframe synchronization ensures that all three components are providing signals of similar significance. Avoid mixing daily Elliott Wave analysis with 15-minute MACD signals and 4-hour RSI readings. Keep your analysis timeframes consistent to maintain proper perspective about signal importance and duration.

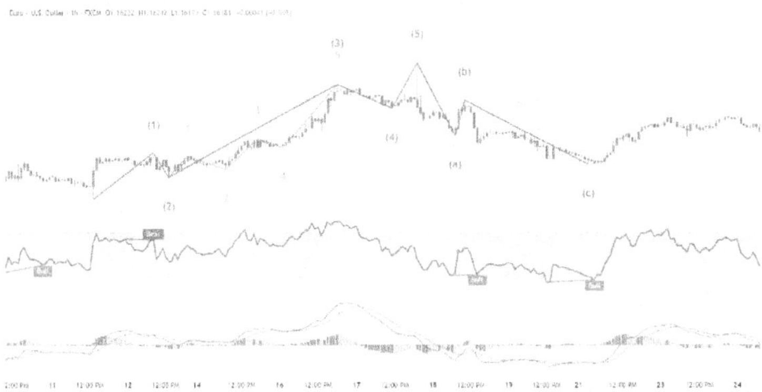

Chart 15: EUR/USD 1-hour chart with three-panel layout showing price action with wave labels in the top panel, MACD with histogram in the middle panel, and RSI with overbought/oversold levels in the bottom panel

Alert systems help you monitor multiple currency pairs efficiently without missing key signal convergences. Set alerts for MACD crossovers, RSI extreme level breaches, and potential Elliott Wave completion points. This systematic monitoring allows you to focus your attention on pairs showing the highest probability setups.

Entry and Exit Timing with Triple Confirmation

Entry timing improves dramatically when you wait for all three components to align rather than acting on single-indicator signals. The ideal entry occurs when Elliott Wave analysis suggests a new impulse wave is beginning, MACD confirms momentum is building in the expected direction, and RSI shows market conditions are favorable for sustained movement.

For bullish entries, look for completed corrective wave patterns coinciding with MACD bullish crossovers and RSI readings below 50 that are starting to turn higher. The combination suggests that selling pressure has exhausted itself and new buying momentum is developing. This convergence often occurs at the beginning of wave 1 in new impulse sequences.

Exit timing becomes more precise when you monitor how the three components begin diverging from each other. As wave 5 develops in an impulse pattern, Elliott Wave theory suggests the trend is approaching completion. When MACD begins showing bearish divergence and RSI reaches extreme overbought levels, the convergence warns that exit time is approaching.

Partial exit strategies work well with this system because different components often reach their signals at slightly different times. You might take partial profits when RSI reaches extreme levels while holding the remainder of your position until MACD shows clear momentum deterioration or Elliott Wave patterns suggest complete exhaustion.

Stop-loss placement becomes more strategic when based on Elliott Wave structure rather than arbitrary percentage levels. Place stops below the low of wave 4 when trading wave 5, or below the beginning of wave 1 when the entire pattern might be invalidated. MACD and RSI help confirm whether your stop level is being approached due to normal wave development or pattern failure.

Case Study: A Complete Trade From Setup to Profit

During the early months of 2021, AUD/USD was developing what appeared to be a complex corrective pattern after a significant decline. The Elliott Wave count suggested that wave C of an ABC correction was approaching completion around the 0.7200 level. This area had provided support previously and represented a logical termination point for the corrective sequence.

MACD was showing signs of bullish divergence as price made lower lows while the indicator formed higher lows. This divergence pattern was developing across multiple swing lows over several weeks, creating a robust signal that momentum was shifting despite continued price weakness.

RSI had reached oversold levels below 25 and was beginning to form higher lows even as price continued declining. The combination of extreme readings and bullish divergence suggested that selling pressure was becoming exhausted and that a reversal was becoming increasingly likely.

The entry signal came when all three components aligned within a 24-hour period. Elliott Wave analysis suggested the correction was complete, MACD crossed above its signal line for the first time in weeks, and RSI broke above 30, confirming that momentum was shifting from bearish to bullish.

The subsequent advance exceeded expectations, with AUD/USD rallying over 600 pips during the following month. The triple confirmation approach provided confidence to hold the position through minor pullbacks that might have otherwise triggered premature exits. MACD remained in bullish territory throughout the advance, confirming the strength of the new trend.

Exit signals began developing as RSI reached overbought levels above 75 and MACD began showing signs of momentum deceleration. Elliott Wave analysis suggested that either wave 1 or wave 3 of the new impulse was approaching completion, providing a logical framework for profit-taking decisions.

Building Systematic Analysis Skills

Developing proficiency with the triple confirmation system requires systematic practice and careful record-keeping. Document each trade setup showing how all three components contributed to your decision-making process. This documentation helps you identify which signal combinations provide the highest success rates and which should be avoided.

Pattern recognition improves when you study both successful and unsuccessful setups. Failed trades often show cases where one component was providing false signals while the others remained neutral or contradictory. Learning to recognize these warning signs helps you avoid marginal setups and focus on the highest-probability opportunities.

The triple confirmation system transforms trading from reactive decision-making to proactive analysis. Instead of chasing price movements or fighting against trends, you learn to anticipate market turning points and position yourself advantageously before major moves develop. This systematic approach leads to more consistent profits and reduced emotional stress in your trading activities.

CONCLUSION

You Now Have a Complete Trading System

The integration of Elliott Wave theory with MACD and RSI indicators creates a robust trading framework that addresses the three critical aspects of successful forex trading: direction, momentum, and timing. You now possess the knowledge to identify where markets are likely to move based on wave structure, confirm that momentum supports your analysis, and time your entries when conditions are optimal for sustained price movement.

The Synergy of Multiple Analysis Methods

What makes this combined approach so powerful is how each component compensates for the weaknesses of the others while amplifying their strengths. Elliott Wave analysis can sometimes leave you uncertain about exact timing, but MACD crossovers and RSI levels provide precise entry signals. Technical indicators occasionally generate false signals in isolation, but Elliott Wave context helps you filter out low-probability setups and focus on high-probability opportunities.

The psychological benefits of this systematic approach cannot be overstated. When all three analytical methods point in the same direction, you trade with confidence rather than hope. This confidence allows you to hold winning positions longer and cut losing trades shorter, which are essential skills for long-term trading success.

During my years of developing and refining this system, I've discovered that the most profitable trades occur when the signals align across multiple timeframes. A weekly

Elliott Wave pattern completion supported by daily MACD divergence and 4-hour RSI extremes creates setup conditions that often lead to sustained trending moves lasting weeks or months.

Understanding Market Context and Adaptation

Successful implementation of this system requires understanding that market conditions constantly evolve, and your analytical approach must adapt accordingly. During strongly trending periods, RSI can remain in extreme territory for extended periods while MACD maintains its directional bias. These conditions favor trend-following strategies based on Elliott Wave impulse patterns.

Conversely, during ranging market conditions, both MACD and RSI tend to oscillate between extreme levels more frequently, making corrective Elliott Wave patterns more common. Recognizing these different market environments helps you adjust your expectations and trading strategies appropriately.

The integration approach also helps you avoid common trading mistakes that plague individual indicator systems. MACD whipsaws become less problematic when filtered through Elliott Wave structure analysis. RSI false signals decrease when you understand the wave context in which they're occurring. Elliott Wave miscounts become apparent when momentum indicators fail to confirm your structural analysis.

Risk Management Through Integrated Analysis

Your risk management improves significantly when based on comprehensive analysis rather than arbitrary rules. Elliott Wave patterns provide natural stop-loss levels based on structural invalidation points, while MACD and RSI help you recognize when those levels are likely to be tested versus when they represent genuine pattern failures.

Position sizing becomes more strategic when you can assess setup quality through multiple analytical lenses. High-confidence trades showing strong Elliott Wave patterns supported by clear MACD momentum and favorable RSI conditions justify larger position sizes. Marginal setups with weak indicator confirmation should receive smaller allocations or be avoided entirely.

The system also helps you manage winning trades more effectively. Elliott Wave targets provide logical profit-taking levels, while MACD momentum deterioration and RSI extreme readings warn when those targets are being approached. This multi-faceted approach to trade management typically results in better average profits per trade.

Building Trading Discipline and Consistency

The systematic nature of this approach naturally builds trading discipline by providing clear criteria for trade selection and management. You're no longer making impulsive decisions based on incomplete analysis or emotional reactions to price movements. Instead, you're following a proven framework that considers multiple aspects of market behavior.

Consistency improves because you're applying the same analytical process to every potential trade opportunity. This standardized approach reduces the impact of subjective judgment while maintaining the flexibility to adapt to different market conditions and currency pair characteristics.

The documentation and analysis skills you develop through this systematic approach also accelerate your learning curve. When you record the Elliott Wave count, MACD signals, and RSI levels for each trade, you create a database of information that reveals which setups work best in different market environments.

Preparing for Advanced Implementation

The foundation you've built through mastering technical integration prepares you for the advanced concepts we'll explore in the final book. You'll learn to apply these principles across multiple timeframes simultaneously, develop sophisticated risk management strategies, and create comprehensive trading plans that account for various market scenarios.

The multi-timeframe analysis techniques we'll cover next build upon your current knowledge by showing how Elliott Wave patterns, MACD signals, and RSI levels interact across different time horizons. This expanded perspective provides even greater precision in timing entries and exits while maintaining the systematic approach you've already learned.

Your understanding of how technical indicators confirm Elliott Wave analysis also prepares you for more complex wave structures and unusual market conditions. The experience you gain from applying this integrated approach will serve as the foundation for handling challenging analytical situations that require flexibility within a structured framework.

Moving Forward with Confidence

You now possess a complete trading system that provides clear signals for entering and exiting forex trades based on sound analytical principles. The combination of Elliott Wave structure, MACD momentum, and RSI timing creates a comprehensive approach that addresses the most common causes of trading losses: poor direction analysis, inadequate momentum confirmation, and terrible timing.

The journey from novice trader to systematic analyst represents a significant achievement that positions you among the minority of market participants who trade based on objective analysis rather than emotional impulses. Your ability to integrate multiple analytical methods while maintaining focus on the most important signals distinguishes your approach from the scattered, inconsistent methods that characterize unsuccessful trading.

This systematic foundation enables you to approach forex markets with confidence and clarity, knowing that your trading decisions are based on proven analytical methods that have stood the test of time across different market conditions and currency pairs.

BOOK 3

Advanced Application and Mastery

Professional-Level Strategies and Real-World Trading Implementation

CHAPTER 1

Advanced Wave Relationships and Extensions

Understanding wave extensions and Fibonacci relationships transforms Elliott Wave analysis from pattern recognition into precise forecasting tool. These advanced concepts allow you to project specific price targets and identify when trends are likely to accelerate beyond normal expectations. The mathematical relationships between waves provide objective measurements that remove guesswork from your trading decisions.

Understanding Wave Extensions in Trending Markets

Wave extensions occur when one of the three impulse waves (1, 3, or 5) becomes significantly longer than the other two waves in the sequence. These extensions represent periods when market psychology becomes extremely one-sided, creating sustained price movements that often exceed trader expectations. In forex markets, wave extensions frequently develop during major economic shifts or central bank policy changes.

Wave 3 extensions are the most common and powerful extensions you'll encounter in currency trading. When wave 3 extends, it typically reaches 1.618 or 2.618 times the length of wave 1, creating dramatic price movements that can last for weeks or months. These extensions often occur when fundamental factors strongly favor one currency over another, such as during interest rate cycles or economic crises.

The psychological driver behind wave 3 extensions lies in the mass recognition phase of trend development. Initial buyers in wave 1 are vindicated by further price movement, attracting additional participants who create the momentum for extended wave 3 development. This self-reinforcing cycle continues until the wave reaches extreme Fibonacci extension levels.

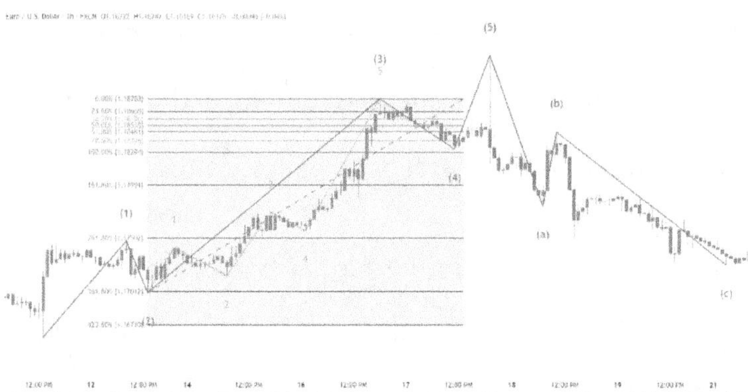

Chart 16: chart showing wave 3 extension reaching 2.618 times wave 1 length with Fibonacci extension levels marked and price targets achieved

Wave 1 extensions are less common but can be equally profitable when identified early. These extensions typically develop when a new trend begins with unusual strength, often following significant fundamental changes or technical breakouts from long-term consolidation patterns. Extended wave 1 patterns suggest that the overall impulse sequence will be powerful and sustained.

Wave 5 extensions create unique trading opportunities because they often conclude with dramatic blow-off moves followed by sharp reversals. These extensions frequently occur when retail traders finally recognize a trend and jump aboard en masse, creating the final push that completes the impulse pattern. Extended wave 5 patterns require careful monitoring because they can reverse suddenly once the extension completes.

Fibonacci Relationships Between Waves

Fibonacci ratios provide objective tools for measuring wave relationships and projecting price targets in Elliott

Wave analysis. These mathematical relationships appear consistently across different timeframes and currency pairs, giving you reliable benchmarks for assessing wave development and planning trading strategies.

The most reliable Fibonacci relationships occur between waves 1 and 3 within impulse patterns. Wave 3 typically measures 1.618, 2.618, or occasionally 4.236 times the length of wave 1. When wave 3 reaches the 1.618 extension, it suggests normal wave development. Extensions to 2.618 or beyond indicate exceptionally strong trending conditions that often continue into wave 5.

Wave 5 projections become more accurate when based on the combined lengths of waves 1 through 3. Common wave 5 targets include 0.618 times the distance from the beginning of wave 1 to the end of wave 3, or equality with wave 1 when projected from the wave 4 low. These relationships help you set realistic profit targets and identify potential reversal zones.

Corrective wave relationships follow their own Fibonacci patterns that help identify correction completion points. Wave C typically equals wave A in length, reaches 1.618 times wave A, or occasionally extends to 2.618 times wave A in strong corrective phases. These relationships help you anticipate where corrective phases are likely to end and new impulse waves begin.

Internal wave relationships within extended waves also follow Fibonacci principles. When wave 3 extends, its internal subdivision often shows the same Fibonacci relationships that appear in larger degree patterns. This fractal nature of Elliott Waves means you can apply the same analytical principles across multiple timeframes simultaneously.

Complex Wave Structures in Major Currency Pairs

Major currency pairs occasionally develop complex wave structures that challenge traditional Elliott Wave interpretation. These patterns typically occur during periods of economic uncertainty when market participants cannot reach clear consensus about currency valuations. Understanding these complex structures prevents misinterpretation of market conditions.

Diagonal patterns represent one type of complex structure that appears in both leading and ending positions within Elliott Wave sequences. Leading diagonals occur in wave 1 or wave A positions, while ending diagonals typically appear as wave 5 or wave C. These patterns consist of five waves that overlap in a converging price channel, creating a wedge-like appearance on price charts.

Double and triple zigzag corrections create another category of complex structures that can confuse wave counting. These patterns link multiple corrective sequences with intervening X waves, creating extended sideways or counter-trend movement. The key to identifying these patterns lies in recognizing that each component maintains its own three-wave internal structure.

Combination corrections blend different corrective patterns into single sequences, such as flat-X-zigzag or triangle-X-flat combinations. These complex corrections often develop when fundamental factors create conflicting pressures that prevent clear directional resolution. Patience becomes essential when trading through these periods because premature position-taking often results in whipsaw losses.

Trading Story: Navigating Extended Wave 3 in GBP/JPY

During the summer of 2022, I was monitoring GBP/JPY after identifying what appeared to be a completed corrective phase around the 155.00 level. The Elliott Wave count suggested that a new impulse wave was beginning, with wave 1 reaching approximately 165.00 before a normal wave 2 correction developed back to 160.50.

The wave 3 development that followed exceeded all normal expectations. Instead of reaching the typical 1.618

extension around 175.00, the wave continued advancing relentlessly. As price broke through 180.00, I realized this was becoming an extended wave 3 that would likely reach much higher levels.

Using Fibonacci extension analysis, I projected potential targets at 2.618 times wave 1, which suggested the 185.00 area as a logical extension target. The wave ultimately peaked around 184.50, demonstrating how Fibonacci relationships can provide accurate price projections even during extreme market conditions.

The key lesson from this experience was learning to adjust expectations when extensions develop. Rather than assuming the wave would complete at normal Fibonacci levels, I allowed the market to show me where the extension would terminate. This flexibility, combined with systematic Fibonacci analysis, allowed me to capture the majority of an exceptional trending move.

Applying Advanced Relationships in Real-Time Analysis

Implementing advanced wave relationships in live trading requires systematic measurement and projection techniques. I recommend creating templates that automatically calculate common Fibonacci extensions and retracements based on completed wave segments. These tools eliminate calculation errors and speed up your analytical process during volatile market conditions.

Multi-timeframe verification strengthens your wave relationship analysis by confirming that projections align across different time horizons. Weekly wave extensions should correlate with daily wave subdivisions, creating consistent targeting across your analytical timeframes. When projections conflict between timeframes, it often indicates that wave counting errors require correction.

The integration of advanced wave relationships with MACD and RSI analysis creates even more powerful forecasting capabilities. Extended waves often show sustained momentum on MACD while RSI may remain in trending territory for extended periods. These indicator patterns help confirm that extensions are developing rather than normal wave completions.

Understanding wave extensions and Fibonacci relationships elevates your Elliott Wave analysis from subjective pattern recognition to objective measurement and projection. These advanced concepts provide the precision needed for professional-level trading while maintaining the systematic approach that generates consistent results across different market conditions and currency pairs.

CHAPTER 2
Multi-Timeframe Elliott Wave Analysis

Mastering multi-timeframe analysis transforms your Elliott Wave trading from reactive decision-making into proactive market anticipation. When you synchronize wave patterns across different time horizons, you gain unprecedented insight into market structure and timing. This sophisticated approach allows you to identify high-probability setups while avoiding the countless false signals that plague single-timeframe analysis.

Synchronizing Waves Across Different Timeframes

The fractal nature of Elliott Wave patterns means that waves subdivide consistently across all timeframes, creating a hierarchical structure that provides multiple layers of analysis. A single wave on the weekly chart contains five complete waves when viewed on the daily timeframe, and each of those daily waves subdivides into five more waves on the hourly charts.

This fractal relationship creates powerful analytical opportunities when properly understood. You can use longer timeframes to identify the overall market direction and major wave position while employing shorter timeframes to pinpoint precise entry and exit timing. The key is maintaining consistency between your wave counts across different time horizons.

Weekly charts provide the macro perspective that prevents you from getting lost in short-term market noise. These longer-term patterns often persist for months or years, giving you the strategic framework for understanding where major currency pairs are positioned in their larger wave cycles. Monthly analysis becomes valuable for identifying multi-year wave patterns that govern long-term currency trends.

Daily charts bridge the gap between strategic weekly analysis and tactical shorter-term timing. The daily timeframe typically provides the clearest Elliott Wave patterns for most forex traders because it filters out excessive noise while maintaining enough detail for practical trading decisions. Most of your primary wave counting should focus on daily patterns supported by weekly context.

Four-hour and hourly charts excel at providing precise timing for entries and exits once you've identified the broader wave structure on longer timeframes. These shorter periods help you avoid entering trades during temporary counter-trend movements and allow you to capture optimal entry points at wave completion levels.

Top-Down Analysis for High-Probability Trades

Effective multi-timeframe analysis always begins with the longest timeframe and works systematically toward shorter periods. This top-down approach ensures that your shorter-term trades align with longer-term wave development rather than fighting against major trends. The process requires discipline because shorter timeframes often tempt you with apparent opportunities that contradict longer-term analysis.

Start your analysis by identifying the current position within major weekly or monthly wave patterns. Are you in an impulse phase or a corrective phase at the highest degree? This determination provides the foundation for all subsequent analysis because it tells you whether to favor trend-following or counter-trend strategies in your shorter-term trading.

Once you understand the major wave position, examine how that pattern is subdividing on daily charts. If the weekly pattern suggests you're in wave 3 of a larger impulse, look for five-wave subdivisions on the daily timeframe that confirm this interpretation. The daily waves should support the weekly count rather than contradicting it.

The final step involves using shorter timeframes to identify optimal entry points within the established wave structure. If daily analysis shows wave 4 correction completing, use hourly charts to pinpoint the exact moment when wave 5 begins developing. This precision timing often means the difference between profitable trades and marginal results.

Confirmation becomes crucial when signals appear across multiple timeframes simultaneously. The highest probability trades develop when weekly patterns, daily subdivisions, and hourly timing all support the same directional bias. These convergence points often produce the most reliable and profitable trading opportunities.

Managing Trades Across Multiple Time Horizons

Position management becomes more sophisticated when based on multi-timeframe wave analysis because different timeframes provide different perspectives on the same price movement. Your stop-loss placement might be based on weekly wave invalidation levels while your profit targets come from daily wave projections and your entry timing relies on hourly patterns.

Stop-loss levels should generally be based on the timeframe that corresponds to your intended holding period. If you plan to hold a position for several weeks based on weekly wave analysis, place your stops at weekly wave invalidation points rather than daily or hourly levels. This approach prevents premature exit due to normal shorter-term fluctuations.

Partial profit-taking strategies work exceptionally well with multi-timeframe analysis because different timeframes often reach completion signals at different times. You might take partial profits when hourly RSI reaches extreme levels while holding the remainder until daily Elliott Wave targets are achieved or weekly momentum begins deteriorating.

Position sizing can be adjusted based on the strength of multi-timeframe confirmation. Trades showing strong alignment across weekly, daily, and hourly analysis justify larger position sizes than those based on single-timeframe signals. This dynamic sizing approach maximizes profits during high-confidence setups while limiting risk during marginal opportunities.

Personal Experience: How Timeframe Analysis Transformed My Trading

My understanding of multi-timeframe analysis developed gradually through years of making timing mistakes based on single-timeframe signals. I would identify beautiful Elliott Wave patterns on daily charts only to enter at precisely the wrong moment because I ignored shorter-term timing factors. Conversely, I would catch perfect hourly entries that immediately reversed because they fought against weekly trends.

The breakthrough came when I started treating each timeframe as providing specific information rather than competing signals. Weekly charts told me which direction to trade, daily charts showed me the wave structure within that direction, and hourly charts gave me precise timing for entries and exits. This systematic approach eliminated most of the conflicting signals that had previously confused my decision-making.

One particularly memorable trade involved AUD/USD during early 2021. Weekly analysis showed the pair completing a major corrective phase that had lasted over a year. Daily charts revealed an ABC correction ending around 0.7200. Four-hour analysis pinpointed the exact moment when wave C completed and a new impulse wave began developing.

The entry came when all timeframes aligned perfectly. Weekly patterns suggested a major reversal, daily waves showed correction completion, and hourly momentum indicators confirmed the directional shift. The subsequent advance lasted over two months and provided multiple opportunities for profit-taking based on shorter-term wave completions within the larger trending move.

Building Multi-Timeframe Analysis Skills

Developing proficiency in multi-timeframe analysis requires systematic practice and careful documentation of how patterns develop across different time horizons. Start by analyzing completed wave sequences retrospectively, tracking how major weekly patterns subdivided into daily waves and how daily patterns broke down into hourly movements.

Software tools can accelerate your learning curve by allowing you to quickly switch between timeframes while maintaining consistent wave labeling. Many platforms offer synchronized charting features that display multiple timeframes simultaneously, making it easier to spot alignment opportunities and timing convergence points.

The most common mistake in multi-timeframe analysis is allowing shorter-term patterns to override longer-term structure. When hourly charts suggest bullish opportunities while weekly patterns indicate major bearish trends, the weekly analysis should take precedence. Learning to maintain this hierarchy prevents costly mistakes that result from fighting against major wave development.

Patience becomes essential when waiting for multi-timeframe alignment because these high-probability setups don't occur daily. However, the improved accuracy and profit potential of properly aligned signals more than compensates for the reduced frequency of trading opportunities. Quality always surpasses quantity in systematic Elliott Wave trading.

Multi-timeframe analysis represents the difference between amateur wave counting and professional market analysis. When you master the ability to synchronize patterns across different time horizons, you join the ranks of traders who consistently profit from Elliott Wave principles rather than occasionally getting lucky with isolated patterns.

CHAPTER 3
Risk Management in Elliott Wave Trading

Effective risk management separates consistently profitable Elliott Wave traders from those who experience dramatic account swings despite accurate pattern identification. The structured nature of Elliott Wave patterns provides natural frameworks for position sizing, stop-loss placement, and profit-taking decisions that significantly improve your long-term trading results.

Position Sizing Based on Wave Analysis

Wave analysis provides objective criteria for determining appropriate position sizes based on setup quality and risk-reward potential. High-confidence wave completions showing strong multi-timeframe alignment justify larger position sizes than marginal patterns with questionable wave counts. This systematic approach to sizing eliminates emotional decision-making while maximizing profits during optimal trading conditions.

The reliability of your wave count directly influences appropriate position sizing. Textbook five-wave impulse patterns with clear subdivisions and proper Fibonacci relationships warrant more aggressive sizing than complex corrective patterns with multiple valid interpretations. When MACD and RSI confirm your Elliott Wave analysis, the convergence of signals supports increased position sizes.

Risk-reward calculations become more precise when based on Elliott Wave targets and invalidation levels.

Wave 3 trades often offer risk-reward ratios exceeding 3:1 because the profit potential extends to 1.618 or 2.618 Fibonacci extensions while stop-losses can be placed at wave 1 highs. These favorable ratios justify larger positions even when your win rate might be lower than simpler trading strategies.

Account percentage rules work best when adjusted for wave pattern reliability rather than applied uniformly across all trades. Reserve your largest position sizes (2-3% account risk) for the clearest wave 3 setups with strong confirmation. Use moderate sizing (1-2% risk) for wave 5 trades and wave completion reversals. Limit your smallest positions (0.5-1% risk) to complex corrective patterns or questionable wave counts.

Correlation considerations become important when trading multiple currency pairs simultaneously. EUR/USD and GBP/USD often move in similar directions, so taking large positions in both pairs simultaneously can create excessive risk concentration. Diversify your Elliott Wave trades across different currency groups to reduce correlation risk while maintaining systematic position sizing.

Stop-Loss Placement Using Wave Structures

Elliott Wave patterns provide logical stop-loss levels based on structural invalidation points rather than arbitrary percentage or pip distances. These natural stop levels often provide better risk-reward ratios while respecting the underlying market structure that drives price movements.

Wave invalidation levels represent the most reliable stop-loss placement because they mark points where your wave count becomes impossible. For wave 3 trades, place stops below the wave 1 high because wave 4 cannot overlap wave 1 in impulse patterns. This structural rule provides objective stop placement that eliminates guesswork from your risk management decisions.

Corrective wave stops follow different principles because corrections can retrace more deeply than impulse waves.

When trading wave C completions, place stops beyond reasonable extension levels such as 1.618 times wave A rather than at specific wave levels. This approach accounts for the more variable nature of corrective patterns while maintaining systematic risk control.

Trailing stop strategies can be adapted to Elliott Wave development by moving stops to protect profits as waves progress. After wave 3 shows clear development, move your stop to breakeven or the wave 2 low to protect against complete profit loss. This approach allows you to participate in extended wave developments while limiting downside risk.

Multiple stop levels work well for larger positions divided into partial units. Use tight stops on portion of your position based on short-term wave subdivisions while maintaining wider stops on the remainder based on major wave invalidation levels. This tiered approach balances profit protection with participation in extended wave developments.

When to Exit Profitable Wave Trades

Profit-taking decisions become more systematic when based on Elliott Wave targets and momentum deterioration rather than arbitrary profit levels or emotional responses to price movements. Different wave positions require different exit strategies because each wave type has distinct profit potential and completion characteristics.

Wave 3 trades offer the greatest profit potential but require patience to capture full extensions. Initial profit-taking can occur at 1.618 extensions of wave 1, with remaining positions held for potential 2.618 extensions. Watch for MACD momentum deterioration and RSI extreme readings to signal when wave 3 might be approaching completion.

Wave 5 completion trades require more aggressive profit management because fifth waves often show momentum divergence and can end abruptly. Take partial profits at equality with wave 1 projected from the wave 4 low, with remaining positions closed when RSI reaches extreme levels or MACD shows clear bearish divergence.

Corrective wave trades typically offer smaller profit potential but higher probability outcomes. Exit ABC correction trades when wave C reaches equality with wave A or 1.618 extensions of wave A. These corrections rarely extend beyond 2.618 times wave A, so aggressive profit-taking becomes appropriate at extended levels.

Time-based exits complement price-based targets by recognizing that waves have typical duration characteristics. Wave 3 developments often last several weeks in daily timeframe analysis, while wave 5 patterns frequently complete more quickly. When wave durations extend significantly beyond normal ranges, it often signals approaching completion regardless of price targets.

My Worst Trading Mistake and the Lesson It Taught Me

The most expensive lesson in my trading career came from ignoring Elliott Wave risk management principles during what appeared to be a perfect wave 3 setup in GBP/USD. The pattern looked textbook perfect, with clear five-wave subdivisions and strong momentum confirmation from both MACD and RSI. My confidence in the setup led me to risk far more than my normal position sizing rules allowed.

The trade initially moved in my favor, advancing over 200 pips within the first week. However, instead of taking partial profits at the first Fibonacci target, I held the entire position expecting the wave 3 to extend to higher levels. When the market suddenly reversed, I discovered that my wave count was wrong - what I thought was wave 3 was actually wave B of a complex correction.

The position quickly moved against me, but my oversized position made it difficult to accept the loss. I violated multiple risk management rules by moving my stop-loss further away and adding to the losing position. The eventual loss exceeded 8% of my account value, far beyond any reasonable risk management guidelines.

This painful experience taught me several critical lessons about Elliott Wave risk management. First, position sizing must remain consistent regardless of setup confidence because even the clearest patterns can be misinterpreted. Second, partial profit-taking at logical targets helps lock in gains while maintaining participation in extended moves. Third, stop-loss levels based on wave invalidation must be respected regardless of temporary paper profits.

The most important lesson was understanding that risk management rules exist precisely for those times when you feel most confident about a trade. Overconfidence leads to oversizing positions and ignoring risk control measures, which inevitably results in account-damaging losses that can take months to recover from.

Systematic Risk Management Implementation

Successful Elliott Wave risk management requires systematic implementation of rules that govern every aspect of trade execution. Document your position sizing criteria, stop-loss placement methodology, and profit-taking strategies to ensure consistent application across all trading opportunities.

Pre-trade analysis should include risk-reward calculations based on Elliott Wave targets and invalidation levels. This analysis helps you determine whether potential trades meet your minimum profitability criteria before committing capital. Trades failing to offer at least 2:1 risk-reward ratios should be avoided regardless of pattern quality.

Regular account reviews help you identify patterns in your risk management implementation that might need adjustment. Track your average win-loss ratios, maximum drawdown periods, and profit-taking effectiveness across different Elliott Wave setups. This data helps you refine your risk management approach based on actual trading results rather than theoretical expectations.

Risk management in Elliott Wave trading ultimately comes down to respecting the probabilistic nature of pattern analysis while systematically managing the inevitable losses that occur when patterns fail to develop as expected. The structured approach transforms trading from gambling into a systematic business with controllable risks and measurable outcomes.

CONCLUSION
Your Journey to Elliott Wave Mastery Continues

You've now reached the pinnacle of systematic Elliott Wave trading education, possessing the advanced skills that separate professional traders from casual market participants. The integration of complex wave relationships, multi-timeframe analysis, and sophisticated risk management creates a comprehensive trading framework that can adapt to any market condition while maintaining consistent profitability over time.

The Professional Trader's Mindset

The transformation from amateur pattern recognition to professional Elliott Wave analysis represents more than just acquiring technical knowledge. You've developed the analytical discipline required to maintain objectivity during volatile market conditions and the patience to wait for high-probability setups rather than forcing marginal trades. This psychological evolution often proves more valuable than any single technical concept.

Professional Elliott Wave trading demands systematic approach to every aspect of market analysis and trade execution. Your ability to synchronize patterns across multiple timeframes while managing risk according to wave structure principles positions you among the elite minority of traders who consistently profit from forex markets. The structured methodology eliminates emotional decision-making while providing clear criteria for evaluating trading opportunities.

The mathematical precision you've learned through Fibonacci relationships and wave extensions transforms subjective pattern interpretation into objective price projection. When combined with MACD momentum confirmation and RSI timing signals, this analytical framework provides unprecedented accuracy in anticipating market behavior. These skills compound over time as your pattern recognition abilities continue developing through practical application.

Continuous Learning and Adaptation

Elliott Wave mastery represents a continuous journey rather than a final destination because markets constantly evolve and present new challenges that test your analytical skills. The foundation you've built provides the flexibility to adapt your approach as market conditions change while maintaining the systematic principles that generate consistent results.

Advanced wave patterns will continue appearing throughout your trading career, each offering opportunities to refine your analytical abilities and expand your understanding of market psychology. Complex corrections, unusual extensions, and multi-month wave developments all contribute to your growing database of pattern recognition experience that improves your future analysis accuracy.

The integration skills you've developed between Elliott Wave theory and technical indicators create a robust analytical framework that can incorporate additional tools and concepts as your trading experience expands. Future learning might include advanced Fibonacci techniques, sector rotation analysis, or fundamental factor integration without disrupting your core systematic approach.

Market environment changes require ongoing adaptation of your analytical emphasis while maintaining core principles. Trending markets favor impulse pattern analysis, while ranging conditions emphasize corrective pattern identification. Your systematic approach provides the flexibility to adjust your focus based on current market characteristics without abandoning proven methodologies.

Building Long-Term Trading Success

The systematic approach you've mastered creates the foundation for long-term trading success through consistent application of proven principles rather than reliance on occasional lucky trades. Your risk management skills protect your capital during inevitable losing streaks while your pattern recognition abilities position you to capture major trending moves when they develop.

Compound growth becomes possible when you maintain systematic discipline over extended periods. Small, consistent profits from high-probability Elliott Wave setups accumulate significantly over months and years, especially when protected by sophisticated risk management techniques. This mathematical advantage distinguishes professional traders from gamblers who rely on home-run trades to generate profits.

The analytical skills you've developed extend beyond individual trade decisions to encompass portfolio management and strategic market positioning. Understanding major wave cycles helps you adjust overall market exposure based on broader economic trends while maintaining tactical flexibility through shorter-term wave analysis.

Practical Implementation Moving Forward

Your continued success depends on maintaining the systematic discipline you've learned rather than abandoning proven methods during challenging market periods. Losing streaks test every trader's resolve, but your comprehensive understanding of Elliott Wave principles provides the confidence to persist through temporary setbacks while maintaining proper risk control.

Documentation and analysis of your trading results accelerates continued learning by revealing patterns in your decision-making that might require adjustment. Track which Elliott Wave setups produce your highest success rates and which market conditions challenge your analytical abilities. This data-driven approach to self-improvement ensures continuous refinement of your trading approach.

Regular study of current market conditions through your Elliott Wave framework keeps your analytical skills sharp while providing opportunities to identify developing patterns before they become obvious to other market participants. The early identification of major wave developments often provides the most profitable trading opportunities with optimal risk-reward characteristics.

The Path Forward

The knowledge you've gained through these three books represents just the beginning of your Elliott Wave trading journey. Each market cycle presents new learning opportunities that deepen your understanding of wave psychology and improve your pattern recognition abilities. The systematic foundation you've built provides the stability to grow your skills without losing sight of proven principles.

Your transformation from someone who might have viewed forex markets as random chaos to a systematic analyst who recognizes predictable patterns represents a significant achievement. The ability to anticipate market behavior through Elliott Wave analysis, confirm your expectations with technical indicators, and manage risk according to wave structure principles places you in an elite category of market participants.

Success in Elliott Wave trading ultimately comes from consistent application of systematic principles rather than seeking perfect trades or trying to capture every market movement. Your comprehensive understanding of wave theory, technical integration, and risk management provides all the tools necessary for long-term profitability.

The challenge now lies in maintaining discipline and continuing to refine your skills through practical application.

The markets will continue providing opportunities for those who approach them with systematic analysis and disciplined risk management. Your Elliott Wave mastery gives you the tools to recognize and capitalize on these opportunities while protecting your capital during inevitable periods of uncertainty. This combination of analytical skill and risk control creates the foundation for sustained trading success across all market conditions.

Your journey to Elliott Wave mastery continues with every chart you analyze and every trade you execute. The principles you've learned will serve you well as you navigate the endless opportunities that forex markets provide to prepared and systematic traders.

www.ingramcontent.com/pod-product-compliance
Lightning Source LLC
LaVergne TN
LVHW022227200926
848481LV00006B/2161
* 9 7 9 8 2 9 5 5 9 8 6 0 9 *